You are a Strong, Brave, Exceptional, Beautiful, Inspiring, Lovely Girl

Self-Love Journal for Teens Girls

PRAGYA TOMAR

ILLUSTRATED BY MICHELA FIORI

@PenMagicBooks LLC

*Dedicated to my
loving grandma, Kamla.
You are missed.*

You yourself, as much
as anybody in the entire
universe, deserve your
love and affection.
- Buddha

ISBN 978-1-952821-14-1 (Paperback)

https://www.PenMagicBooks.com

PenMagic Books provides special discounts when
purchased in larger volumes for premiums and promotional
purposes, as well as for fundraising and educational use.
Custom editions can also be created for special purposes.
In addition, supplemental teaching material can be
provided upon request.

_ /_ /_

Hey Girl!

My name is Pragya, and I wrote this journal for you. As girls, we are taught
to focus on presenting ourselves in a manner pleasing to others. This journal
allows you to open up, express your innermost thoughts and dreams, and start
a loving dialogue with yourself. I am hopeful that as you go through this book,
the suggested ideas will be inspiring as well as transformative. Some of the
prompts and activities may feel overwhelming at times. However, they will
allow you to dig deeper into your soul, help resolve problems, and make room for
new beginnings. They will provide the support and encouragement needed to be
happy, hopeful, and confident.

When we hear people talk about love, how often do we think about our primary
relationship, the one with ourselves — the one at the heart of everything else?
Pause for a moment to reflect on how you feel about yourself...
Do you love yourself? And what does that even mean?

During my younger years, I wasted my precious time criticizing myself for not
being perfect. But when I learned to accept and embrace myself, my life changed!
The incredible changes I have felt from my self-love journey are more than I
could have ever asked. Self-love breeds self-confidence, self worth, self respect,
and self forgiveness. Do not underestimate the power of self-love. You have to
love yourself before you can ever truly love anyone else, and this journal should
serve as a reminder to always appreciate yourself. The self love quotes and ideas
suggested in the journal are to show you just how awesome you are from the
inside out! Self- confidence is a super power. Once you start to believe in yourself,
and love yourself, magic follows.

Take off your mask, and make some time from your busy schedule. Grab a coffee,
and pamper yourself with this journal. I am truly grateful to you for trusting
me in your journey to explore and discover the best version of yourself.

Much love, hope, and gratitude,
Pragya

What if you simply devoted this year to loving yourself more?

_/_/_

Color this page

Start now.

Start where you are.

Start with fear.

Start with pain.

Start with doubt.

Start with shaking hands.

Start with trembling voice, but start.

Start and don't stop.

Start where you are with what you have.

Start your Journey to

Self-love

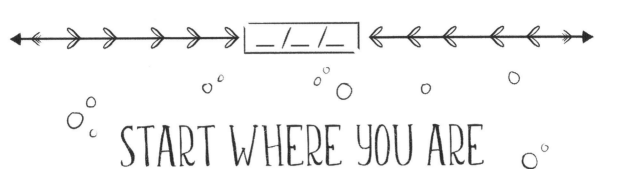

START WHERE YOU ARE

Hey Girl! To achieve anything in life, start where you are. The first step of your journey might be intimidating, but it's also full of excitement and opportunities. It is full of great promise of what could happen, and faith that whatever is meant to happen, will happen. Don't wait for everything to be perfect. Accept and embrace where you are in your journey, even if it's not where you want to be. There is a purpose to everything that happens in our lives. You don't have to know what comes next. You don't have to have everything figured out right this moment. You don't need to know your entire story.

You are a living, changing, growing soul, riding through your unique and beautiful journey of life. And that's exactly what it is— a journey— and it wouldn't be a journey if you knew everything that was coming next. It wouldn't be a journey if you knew how it will all turn out in the end. So be patient with yourself and smile at the unknown, because your story is just starting to be written.

Self-love will heal you, empower you, restore you, and open up new worlds within you and all around you.

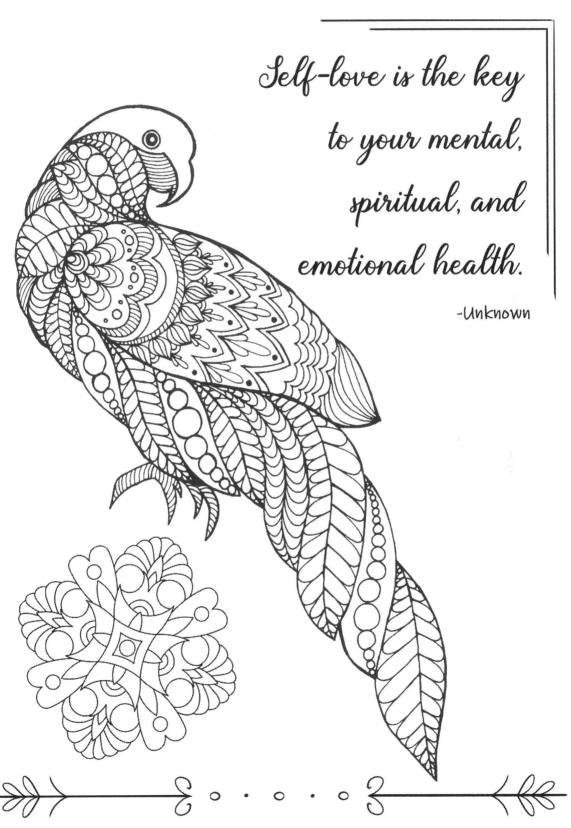

Self-love is the key to your mental, spiritual, and emotional health.

-Unknown

I LOVE MYSELF

"How you love yourself is how you teach others to love you."

- Rupi Kaur

Hey Girl!

When you love yourself, you glow from the inside. You attract people who love, respect, and appreciate your energy. Everything starts with you and how you feel about yourself. Eat like you love yourself. Move like you love yourself. Speak like you love yourself. Act like you love yourself. Loving yourself starts with liking yourself, which starts with respecting yourself, which starts with thinking about yourself in positive ways. You, as much as anybody else, deserve your love and affection. Encourage yourself, believe in yourself, and love yourself. Never doubt who you are. Spend time learning who you are. After all, the only person you're ever going to truly live with is yourself.

When I was young, all of my flaws were blown up in my mind. I flinched at my childhood pictures because I loathed the way I looked. I was so trapped in the idea of not being perfect that I cared less about who I was, and more about who I believed I was ultimately going to be. I told myself that one day I would fix everything that troubled me about myself and become some perfect version of myself who was great and successful in life.

Now, looking back, the only real difference between the person I was when I was younger and the person I am now is that I no longer criticize myself day and night about my imperfections anymore. I've come to love and accept myself for who I am.

The incredible changes in my life that I have felt from my self-love and self-acceptance journey are more than I could have ever asked for. I didn't realize that loving myself would more than satisfy my need to feel validated all the time. Once I began the journey to self-love, my confidence fueled my every move.

Most girls have unrealistic expectations of perfection, many of which are self-imposed. Self-love does not mean one has to be perfect, nor is it always being happy. It is not based on outside validation and measures of success. It does not dwell in shame-based criticism or fear.

Self-love is what gleams through even when we don't accomplish our goals or meet our measurements of success. Self-love involves extending compassion and grace to ourselves, no matter the outcome. Self-love, once realized, allows an individual to reach their full potential, and is filled with empathy, grace, and kindness. Making room and prioritizing ourselves allows us to embrace our lives completely and wholeheartedly.

Self-love is learning to extend compassion toward ourselves, even when we struggle and suffer. Self-Love is forgiving ourselves when we make mistakes. Self-love means prioritizing ourselves and letting ourselves find trust in our strengths and talents. Sometimes it means putting ourselves first. Sometimes it means making room to recognize our needs and desires. It involves having boundaries, and sometimes having boundaries can disappoint others.

When things change inside you,
       things change around you.

You deserve to be here
as much as the trees,
the stars, and the moon.

Your value
doesn't decrease
based on someone's
inability to see
your worth.

Self-love
and
acceptance
reminders

"Worthy now.
Not if. Not when.
We are worthy of love
and belonging now.
Right this minute.
As is."
- Brene Brown

Remember that
when you were born
you were called
a miracle.
You still are that
miracle NOW!

"You are valuable
just because you exist.
Not because of what
you do, or what you
have done, but simply
because you ARE."
- Max Lucado

Color this page

_ /_ /_

Practicing self-love means learning how to trust ourselves, to treat ourselves with respect, and to be kind and affectionate to ourselves.

-Brené Brown

SELF-LOVE QUESTIONNAIRE

Do you believe you are worthy and deserving of love?

_____

_____

Do you believe you are special?

_____

_____

Do you believe you have a purpose for living?

_____

_____

Are you able to communicate your needs and desires?

_____

_____

Do you accept and love your body just the way it looks?

_____

_____

Do you rely on others to feel whole?

_____

_____

Do you believe your feelings matter as much as everyone else's?

_____

_____

_ /_ /_

Do you believe you need to be perfect to be loved?

_____

_____

Do you believe you are worthy of good things in life?

_____

_____

_____

Are you as kind to yourself as you are to other people?

_____

_____

_____

Do you feel guilty if you take care of yourself or do something for yourself?

_____

_____

_____

When you feel lonely, do you tell yourself that no one likes you?

_____

_____

_____

When you make a mistake, are you able to forgive yourself and move on?

_____

_____

_____

Are you too hard on yourself and blame yourself for everything?

_____

_____

Nothing has transformed my life more than realizing that it's a waste of time to evaluate my worthiness by weighing the reaction of the people in the stands. - Brené Brown

_ / _ / _

It's time to:

Love yourself,   Respect yourself,

Admire yourself,   Forgive yourself,

Accept yourself,

Nurture yourself,

Today is the day!

WHO ARE YOU?

In order to discover who we are and why we act the way we do, we have to know our own story. Being brave and willing to explore our life is an important step on the road to understanding ourselves and becoming who we want to be. When we consciously allow and accept who we are to our core and what we desire most in this world, we find that we can be more open, authentic, and honest to our friends and family. Who are you? That is sometimes a really hard question for many of us to answer. You are on your own unique journey to becoming more self-aware, and you deserve to be heard.

Fill out these prompts with first thing that comes to mind.

I am someone who...

Loves
_____

_____

Has the goal of
_____

Is driven by
_____

Who notices
_____

_____

Is happiest when
_____

_____

Wishes I could
_____

_____

Would give
_____

_____

_ / _ / _

Wants to

Used to be afraid of

Is inspired by

Has a habit of

Gets disappointed by

Believes in

Will one day

Is grateful for

Is really good at

Appreciates

Dreams of

After filling these out, think about these beautiful parts of who you are, and share them with those closest to you. Ask them some of the same questions to help get to know them a little better too.

My First

Best friend:

Love:

TV show:

Book:

Boyfriend/Girlfriend:

Record/cd:

Job:

Crush:

Car:

Holiday:

School:

Kiss:

Teacher:

Alcoholic drink:

Sport:

Camping trip:

Secret adventure:

_ / _ / _

ONE WORD

My job:

My happiness:

My love:

My friend:

My parents:

My Music:

My body:

My childhood:

My sibling:

My turn on:

My turn off:

My fear:

My passion:

My guilt:

My addiction:

My hero:

My sanctuary:

I ACCEPT MYSELF

"Because one believes in oneself, one doesn't try to convince others. Because one is content with oneself, one doesn't need others' approval. Because one accepts oneself, the whole world accepts him or her." -Lao Tzu

Hey Girl! You don't need anyone's affection or approval in order to be good enough. When someone rejects, abandons, or judges you, it isn't actually about you. It's about them and their own insecurities, limitations, and needs, and you don't have to internalize that. Your worth isn't contingent upon other people's acceptance of you - it's something inherent.

There is a critical voice inside our head that we hear time and again; the voice that tells us "no body likes me". This critical inner voice starts to take shape early in our lives. It's built out of hurtful negative attitudes that we were exposed to in childhood, especially from significant caretakers. If a parent thought of us as lazy, useless or as a troublemaker, for example, we incorporate these attitudes toward ourselves on a sub-conscious level throughout our lives. We are influenced by how our parents felt about themselves. If they felt awkward socially or had low self-esteem, we take on some of their self-inflicted perceptions as our own. Add to this the many other experiences we had where we felt put down, shamed or rejected—a teacher who humiliated us in front of our class, a bully at school who put us down on a daily basis—and we can start to see how our inner critic took shape.

You exist, and therefore, you matter. You're allowed to voice your thoughts and feelings. You're allowed to assert your needs. You're allowed to take up space. You're allowed to hold on to the truth that who you are is exactly enough. And you're allowed to remove anyone from your life who makes you feel otherwise.

WHO SHAPED YOUR INNER CRITICAL VOICE?
Look back and think about people or events that may have
helped create the inner critical voice that you hear in your mind.
Think about situations that might have stood out as
defining moments in your development. This "critical inner voice"
exists in all of us, reminding us constantly that we aren't good
enough and don't deserve what we desire.

_____

_____

_____

_____

_____

_____

_____

_____

_____

_____

_____

_____

_____

_____

_____

_____

_____

_ / _ / _

Remember,
you have
been criticizing
yourself
for years and
it hasn't worked.
Try approving of
yourself and see
what happens.

- Louise L Hay

As the acceptance of yourself
becomes more important,
the opinions of others
become less important.

When I accept myself,
I am freed from the burden
of needing you to accept me.

Self-Love vs Self-Indulgence

Hey Girl! what is self-love anyway? Is it pedicures? Is it having a glass of wine? Is it that piece of cake you've been denying yourself? No it's not, and here's why. When it comes to self-love, it's a matter of how you feel about yourself. Self-love includes demonstrating maturity, understanding, and compassion for yourself. You demonstrate self-love by taking time to understand your feelings and their impact. You empathize with your heart, showing you understand it. Your compassion is reflected in your attitude of acceptance.

SELF-LOVE	SELF-INDULGENCE
Creating space for your feelings	Creating distraction
Sustained joyful attitude	Momentary happiness
Freedom & power to be yourself	Addiction & dependence
Rooted in authenticity	Rooted in stereotypes
Heart-balanced	Seeking validation from others

while self-indulgence may feel like self-love or self-care, it's usually a way to avoid dealing with your feelings. Things like going shopping, drinking with friends, taking a nap, or treating yourself to a pedicure are really all ways we avoid facing our feelings. Self-indulgence is not bad, and can some-times help you take the step to self-love, but it is important to know the difference. Those things that provide instant gratification often require that we deny or ignore our truth in some way, We become willing to trade our self-love for self-indulgence. In pursuing indulgence over practicing love, we teach ourselves that joy is scarce and fleeting.

Self-love is a real process of choosing what is best for you. It doesn't happen overnight and requires getting to know yourself. But also by loving yourself you are going to accept life as it unfolds, without trying to con-stantly solve or fix things. That's how you are going to accept where you are and begin to value your journey.

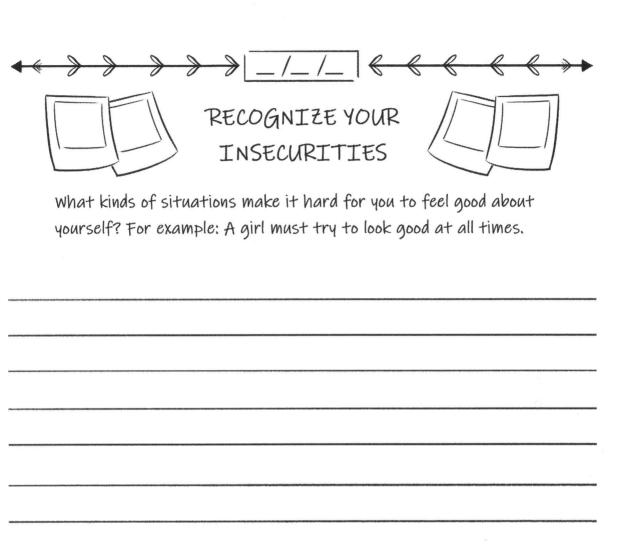

RECOGNIZE YOUR INSECURITIES

What kinds of situations make it hard for you to feel good about yourself? For example: A girl must try to look good at all times.

_____

_____

_____

_____

_____

_____

_____

_____

_____

_____

_____

_____

_____

What are some kind things that you would love to have someone say to you? Take some time to think back and remember kind words that have made a difference to you in the past. Perhaps they boosted your spirits when you were down, or reminded you that you are loved. Look in the mirror and say a few of these messages to yourself. Notice how hearing these positive things makes you feel.

_____

_____

_____

_____

_____

_____

_____

_____

_____

_____

_____

_____

_____

Some people find it hard to spend a few minutes on loving themselves. The shadows of shame whisper that it is selfish or that others need you. Give yourself permission to be loving with yourself. Write a permission slip to yourself and sign it.

_____

_____

_____

_____

_____

_____

Think about an aspect of yourself you have a hard time accepting. It can be a physical characteristic, a behavior, or a personality trait that you have struggled with. Journal about the emotions and thoughts you have about that issue. Practice awareness as you do so. Examine whether you feel drawn to bully yourself or to be kind. Just notice.

_____

_____

_____

_____

I LET GO OF THINGS THAT NO LONGER SERVE ME

"When I let go of what I am, I become what I might be." -Lao Tzu

Hey Girl! Never ruin a good day by thinking about a bad day yesterday. You can spend minutes, hours, days, weeks, or even months over-analyzing a situation; trying to put the pieces together, imagining what could've happened... or you could just leave the pieces on the floor and move on. Don't be afraid to walk away from things, places, and people that leave your soul heavy. Be mindful of where your thoughts are going. Stop re-playing troubling memories from the past. Stop obsessing about the future. Breathe. Be present. Then think of one thought or habit you can do to feel better right here in this moment. Every morning we are born again. What we do today is what matters most.

Recognize when a phase, job, life stage or relationship is over and let it go. Allow yourself to gracefully exit situations you have outgrown. Moving on doesn't have to be a catastrophic event. You can simply move on with peace and clarity.

Starting today, let's try to let go of what's gone, appreciate what still remains, and look forward to what's coming next. Life teaches us the art of letting go. When you have learnt to let go, you will be joyful, and as you start being joyful, more will be given to you.

Accept what is,

Let go of what was.

Have faith in what will be.

LOOKING AT THE PAST

___/___/___

What is one thing that you really need to let go of? How has it affected your present? What did you learn from it?

_____

_____

_____

_____

_____

_____

_____

_____

_____

_____

_____

_____

_____

_____

_____

_____

_____

_____

_____

_____

_/_/_

Comparisons

Painful Past

Perfectionism

Jealousy

Hate

Self-Doubt

I let go of things that do not serve my life.

LOOKING BACK

My earliest memory:

_____

_____

_____

The person I loved the most:

_____

_____

_____

The person who had the greatest impact on me:

_____

_____

_____

As a child, I dreamt of becoming:

_____

_____

_____

My childhood described in one word:

_____

_____

_____

Poster I had on my wall while growing up:

_____

_____

_____

People in history I admire most:

_____

_____

_ / _ / _

The music I loved as a child:

_____

_____

_____

When I look at the past, the thing I miss the most:

_____

_____

_____

The first thing I bought with my own money:

_____

_____

_____

The sport I played when I was a child:

_____

_____

_____

The happiest moment when I was a child:

_____

_____

_____

The hardest thing I have ever done:

_____

_____

_____

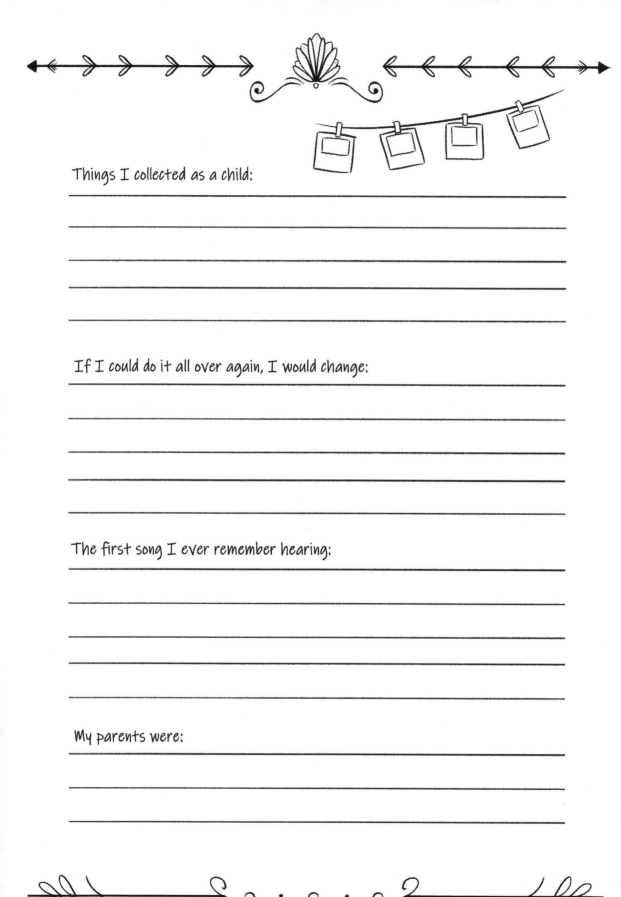

Things I collected as a child:

_____
_____
_____
_____
_____

If I could do it all over again, I would change:

_____
_____
_____
_____
_____

The first song I ever remember hearing:

_____
_____
_____
_____
_____

My parents were:

_____
_____
_____
_____

_ / _ / _

The one thing I regret in the whole world:

_____

_____

_____

_____

The things I am addicted to:

_____

_____

_____

_____

_____

My happiest memory I have:

_____

_____

_____

_____

The book that had the greatest influence on me:

_____

_____

_____

I AM ENOUGH

"And I would find myself again. Not the same version of me that I was looking for, but a stronger version. A wiser version. A woman who knew that she was enough, just as she was. A woman who had been tried in the fire but instead of being burned by it, came out gold. A woman who finally, after doubting and questioning and striving and hustling for her worth for years . . . finally, finally came to the realization that she was and is and has always been . . . enough."

—MANDY HALE

Hey Girl!

You have what it takes. You are strong enough, brave enough, and capable enough. You are worthy. It's time to stop thinking otherwise and start believing in yourself. No one else has the dreams that you have. No one else sees the world exactly like you do, and no one else holds the same magic inside. It's time to start believing in the power of your dreams. Hey Girl, Not next year, not next month, not tomorrow, but now. You are ready.

You are enough.

_ /_ /_

Affirmations to cultivate self-love:

Repeat these every night before sleeping.

I am worthy of loving and being loved.

I trust myself.

I radiate confidence, self-respect, and inner harmony.

I am kind to myself.

I surround myself with good, positive, and supportive people.

I consciously release the painful past and live in the present.

I am grateful for the blessings in my life.

I attract love into my life.

I am beautiful just the way I am.

I accept others and I accept myself.

I choose to stop apologizing for being me.

I release negative self-talk.

I express unconditional love for my mind, body, and soul.

I feel good about myself and the decisions I make.

I love and respect myself deeply.

I am a happy person who has many hopes and dreams.

I am proud of myself and how far I have come.

I deserve to be happy and healthy.

I love my body. I am taking care of my body.

I choose me. I am enough.

My voice is valuable and my opinions matter.

I am creating a beautiful life.

Care about what other
people think and you will
always be their prisoner.
   - Lao Tzu

Stay rooted in your
inner island of serenity.
Don't give power to
external things.

To be enlightened doesn't mean
that you won't have any negative
thoughts. It means
that even while entangled in
these thoughts, you allow them
to come and go without
believing in them
and they dissolve.

—♡—♡—♡—♡—♡—♡—

In the depth of your being,
under the stormy surface
of your mind, under
all the stories you
think you are,
there is a vast ocean
of perfect peace.

I AM CHANGING,

but not in the way you'd expect.
I am changing how I view myself.
I am changing how I talk to myself.
I am changing what I allow, and who I allow in my life.
But most of all... I am no longer changing myself for others;
the pressure to fit in and be anything other than myself.
I am creating a revolution in my own self-care. -Moule T

Hey Girl, You are changing for the better. Know your worth , don't be afraid of losing people — be afraid of losing yourself trying to please everyone around you. It's not about who you used to be, rather about who you wish to be. And it's okay if you don't know how to feel, if you don't know what you want, and if you can't figure out things as you go. It's okay to not want something you worked so hard on getting after realizing it wasn't what you thought it was. It's okay to change your mind, to make mistakes, to walk away from someone you once loved — from something that once meant the world to you. It's okay, because this is your life, your cause, your body, your beliefs, your mind, your heart, and your feelings. And you don't need validation from anyone other than you.

Change can be beautiful and scary at the same time. You can be hurting, and wondering what tomorrow will bring. But you can be healing and happy. Sometimes it's best not to question why you're feeling this way, but instead experience all of the emotions change may bring....

_ / _ / _

THAT ONE CHANGE NEEDED

Describe the one positive change that, if it happens, would make your life better. Why would it make it better?

_____

_____

_____

_____

_____

_____

_____

_____

_____

_____

_____

_____

_____

_____

_____

_____

_____

_____

_____

_____

PERSONAL GROWTH

What do I need more of in my life?

_____

_____

_____

_____

_____

What do I need to let go of? (Fears, toxic energy, relationships)

_____

_____

_____

_____

_____

What are some of my limiting beliefs that might be holding me back?

_____

_____

_____

_____

_ / _ / _

What are five things I am grateful for today?

_____

_____

_____

_____

Where do I see myself in five years?

_____

_____

_____

_____

What unhealthy habits do I need to cut out?

_____

_____

_____

_____

What do I love most about myself?

_____

_____

_____

_____

What does my ideal day look like?

_____

_____

_____

_____

What do I struggle with most?

_____

_____

_____

_____

What motivates me and keeps me going?

_____

_____

_____

_____

What is something I've been wanting to do but am afraid to try? (Why am I afraid?)

_____

_____

_____

If money wasn't an issue, what would my ideal life be?

_____
_____
_____
_____

How can I add happiness to my daily life?

_____
_____
_____
_____

What are three of my life passions?

_____
_____
_____
_____

What are my top three goals for this year and how can I achieve them?

_____
_____
_____
_____

Notes to myself

You deserve happiness. And I mean real happiness; true happiness. The kind of happiness that makes your heart fill with warmth. And you deserve to feel what it feels like to be okay. To feel like the world isn't against you. To feel like you aren't constantly treading water just to keep from drowning. More than anything, you deserve to be okay.

—♡—♡—♡—♡—♡—♡—

I'm not perfect and I don't have to be. When I first realized this I felt an intense relief. This realization allowed me to actually become a better person. It gave me the strength to embrace my flaws and learn from my mistakes. The pressure melted away. I wouldn't have been able to start examining my mistakes if I felt like I had to be perfect. Once I found out it was okay to be imperfect, everything changed for the better.
Goal: Don't criticize yourself for making mistakes— just be conscious not to make the same mistake twice.

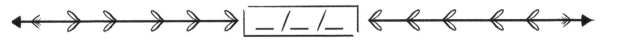
"Today I practice...
Celebrating the success of others.
I practice being genuinely excited and
happy for others when they have wins in
their lives. In fact, I am so supportive of
their success that I celebrate it as if it were
my own. It's a reminder to me that there's
more than enough to go around. It also
reminds me that I am my only competition.
To think of other people as my competitors
means I'm measuring myself with sticks
that belong to others...and I have my own
stick. By practicing this, I can slowly
transform my jealousy and envy into
inspiration and possibilities. When others
are successful at something it means that
it's humanly possible, so it's possible for me too.
By celebrating the success of others
I'm able to move out of competition and
into collaboration. Success leaves clues that
I'm keen to learn. Today I celebrate you."
- Ranbir Puar

—♡—♡—♡—♡—♡—♡—

"This is the part of my life where I silently remove
myself from anyone who hurts me more than they love
me, drains me more than they replenish me, bring me
more stress than they do peace, and try to stunt my
growth rather than applaud it. I think that
I've done more than enough talking and trying
to make things work with certain people...
I'm done."
- Cici.b | The Crimson Kiss

I AM MINDFUL

Wherever you are, be there totally. - Buddha

Mindfulness is the intentional, accepting and non-judgmental focus of one's attention on the emotions, thoughts, and sensations occuring in the present moment.

Hey Girl! Mindfulness is being aware, living in the moment, focusing on breathing, and paying attention to your thoughts as they emerge. Our lives are shaped by our minds, for we become what we choose to think. Your mind will believe everything you tell it. Feed your mind with good thoughts. Feed it the truth. Feed it with care. Some days stink. Not everything is going to be how you want it. You'll get upset. But you can manage this feeling. You can slow down, take a few deep breaths, and pay attention to your feelings.

Hey Girl! You need to know that whatever you are feeling is okay. Listen to your body. Notice your sensations. Pay attention to your mind talking. Are the words supportive and understanding or rude? Are you being gentle to yourself? Let your breath be infused with gratefulness. Be thankful that you can breathe, eat, walk, focus, ask questions, and meditate. This is how we practice mindfulness. This is how we become aware of our minds.

Feelings come and go like clouds in a windy sky.
Conscious breathing is my anchor.
- Thich Nhat Hanh

watch your thoughts like
raindrops

Being aware of your breath forces you into the
present moment—the key to all inner transformation.
Whenever you are conscious of your breath, you are
absolutely present. You may also notice that you
cannot think and be aware of your breathing.
Conscious breathing stops your mind.
- Eckhart Tolle

Aspects of mindfulness practice

Letting go of comparison

Staying Calm

Letting go of judgment

Seeing clearly

Making friends

Listening to your heart

Being fully present

Being aware of your feelings

_ / _ / _

Breathing deep

Allowing everything to belong

Being patient

Honoring yourself

Cultivating positive thinking

Paying attention to your surroundings

Relaxing
Relaxing
Relaxing

I AM GRATEFUL

"Acknowledging the good that you already have in your life is the foundation for all abundance." - Eckhart Tolle

Hey Girl! Gratitude helps you fall in love with the life you already have. Life is short, and we spend so much time sweating small stuff: worrying, comparing, wishing, wanting, and waiting for something bigger and better instead of focussing on all the simple blessings that surround us everyday. Take a step back, and look at all those great things you already have. Too often we underestimate the power of a touch, a smile, a kind word, a listening ear, an honest compliment, or the smallest act of caring. All of these have the potential to turn a life around. It's through the practice of gratitude that we discover happiness, peace, and contentment in our hearts and our lives.

Living with gratitude is a choice you make everyday. It's embracing the gift of life, and recognizing the beauty that is both around and within you. A grateful heart enables you to rise above life's challenges and remain open to growth and opportunities to make a difference in the worlds around you.

Gratitude creates the most wonderful feeling. It can resolve disputes. It can strengthen friendships. And it makes us better human beings.

"Wear gratitude like a cloak
and it will feed every corner
of your life."
- Rumi

"Wake at dawn with a
winged heart and
give thanks for another
day of loving."
- Khalil Gibran

Things I am grateful for:

A strength of mine for which I'm grateful:

_____

Something money can't buy that I'm grateful for:

_____

Something that comforts me that I'm grateful for:

_____

Something that's funny for which I'm grateful:

_____

Something in nature that I'm grateful for:

_____

Something that changes that I'm grateful for:

_____

A memory I'm grateful for:

_____

A challenge I'm grateful for:

_____

Something beautiful that I'm grateful for:

_____

_ / _ / _

Things I love

Write and draw the things you love in the hearts below.

I love...

I love reading...

I love playing...

I love doing...

I love making...

I love eating...

I love watching...

I AM RESILIENT

"Resilience is knowing that you are the only one
that has the power and the responsibility
to pick yourself up." - Mary Holloway

—♡—♡—♡—♡—♡—♡—

She was unstoppable, not because she did not have failures or
doubts, but because she continued on despite them. - Beau Taplin

—♡—♡—♡—♡—♡—♡—

When we learn how to become resilient, we learn how to embrace the
beautifully broad spectrum of the human experience. - Jaeda Dewalt

—♡—♡—♡—♡—♡—♡—

Hey Girl! Resilience is knowing that you are the only one who has
the power and the responsibility to pick yourself up when you fall.
You can overcome the challenges you may be facing. Learn from your
setbacks and mistakes. We all know that obstacles are a part of
your success. Believe me, you are going to be okay. Sometimes the
journey can be longer than expected, but be patient, everything will
work out. Each step takes you closer to your goal. Have a positive
state of mind and don't give up. Because the truth is too many
people quit before even giving themselves a real chance.
Hey Girl, remember that all good things take time. Be patient,
and your time will come too.

Affirmations

I am resilient.

My mind, body, and spirit are strong. I embrace all life's challenges. I experience fear at times just like anyone else, but I refuse to let it define me. I believe positive thinking matters, but that I will succeed through planning, hard work, and determination. I choose happiness each day. I believe in the power of hope. I live my life with trust and courage.

I am resilient.

I make time to reflect, rest, and recharge. I ignore doubters and naysayers especially if they are in my head. I continually nudge my comfort zone because I refuse to live a life that is simply good enough. I believe that love and compassion are necessities, not luxuries. I trust that no matter what happens in my life, I will be okay because I am resilient.

Currently. what are your biggest three goals?

_____

_____

_____

_____

_____

What did you do today to be closer to achievening them?

_____

_____

_____

_____

_____

What change can you make today to be one step closer to those goals?

_____

_____

_____

_____

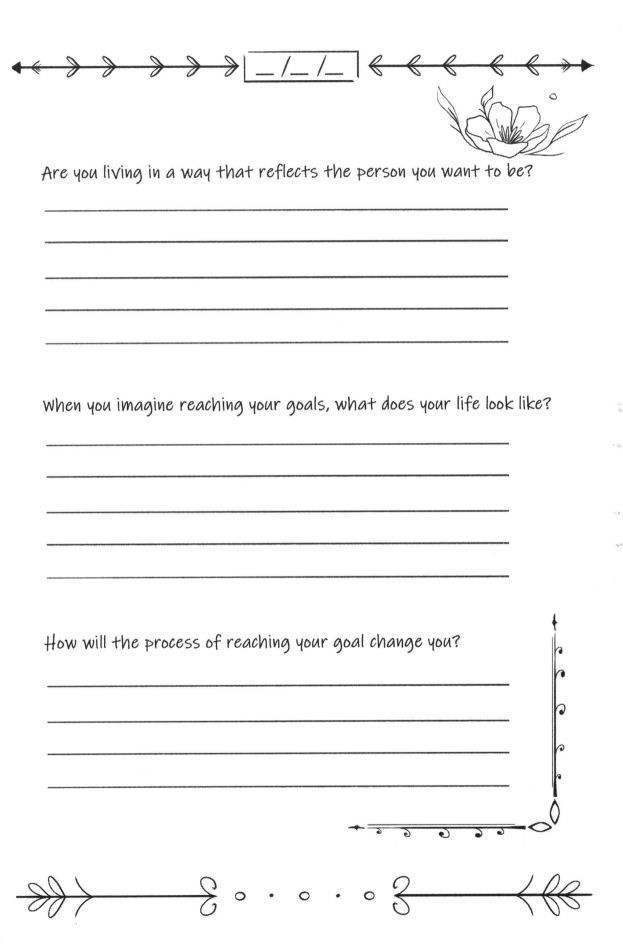

_ /_ /_

Are you living in a way that reflects the person you want to be?

_____
_____
_____
_____
_____

When you imagine reaching your goals, what does your life look like?

_____
_____
_____
_____
_____

How will the process of reaching your goal change you?

_____
_____
_____
_____

_ /_ /_

It's okay
to be yourself,
to make mistakes,
to give yourself time,
to do your own thing,
to know your self-worth,
to give yourself attention,
to do what's best for you,
to give yourself power,
to think differently,
to love youself,
to never give up,
to be okay!

I LIVE IN THE PRESENT

If you want to conquer anxiety of life, live in
the moment, live in the breath. - Amit Ray

Hey Girl! If our minds hold thoughts about the past or the
future, we are not truly loving the present. Stay here, be
present in this moment. Replaying broken memories causes
anger and distress. Worrying about the future creates
anxiety. Practice staying in the present. It will heal you.
Living in the present is the best practice to live your life
peacefully.

Enjoy where you are now. You are supposed to be right
where you are. We are guilty of dwelling on negative
thoughts about our lives. We get trapped into "where should
we be" and all that does is cause stress and anxiety. Stay
here. Stay present. Love this moment. Love yourself as you
are.

—♡—♡—♡—♡—♡—♡—

Let's try staying engaged in the now.

Breath by breath,
let go of the expectation,
fear, regret and frustration.
Let go of the need for
constant approval.
You don't need any of it. - Surya Das

_ _/_ _/_ _

Do not dwell in the past. Do not dream of the future,
Focus the mind on the present moment. - Buddha

Your mind puts conditions on your happiness. It doesn't want you to be happy now. It wants you to be happy when...

Today I am at peace and my mind will no longer over-analyze the past or stress about the unknown future. I am present in the moment in front of my eyes.

I AM PRESENT

Color them as you experience them

Connect with nature

Drink water

Have a picnic in the backyard

Look at the stars

Set a daily intention

Go for a long walk

Breathe deeply

Read a favorite book

Take a digital break

Define three daily goals

Watch the sunset

Enjoy a warm bath

Read inspirational content

Stretch

Light a candle

Create a tea or coffee ritual

Recite positive affirmations

Eat ice from a cup

Awaken with gratitude

Cultivate humility

Laugh

Notice your thoughts

Practice shower meditation

Make your bed mindfully

Declutter one space

Eat breakfast mindfully

Practice morning meditation

Write in a journal

Stand, stretch, and get moving

AFFIRMATIONS TO LIVE IN THE PRESENT

Today will be a good day.

Everything will be okay.

I am in control

of my life and feelings.

I have people that love me.

I have a lot to be grateful for.

Everything I need is within me.

Tomorrow will be better.

_ /_ /_

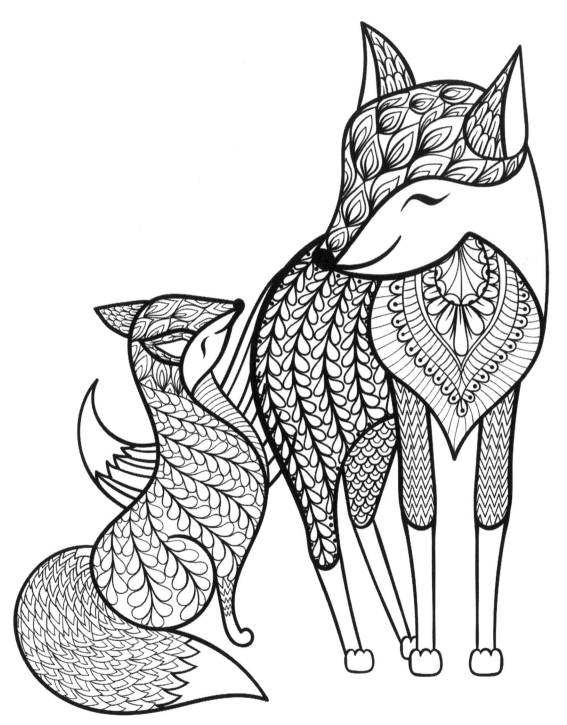

What I do know...

"Imagine you are a lake...
the surface of the lake changes according
to weather, wind, rain etc...

But the depth of the lake remains always
undisturbed. The depth of the lake is your
inner state, not dependent on external things."
- Eckhart Tolle

I AM CALM

I can manage my emotions in tough situations.

—♡—♡—♡—♡—♡—♡—

Hey Girl! When you can't control what's happening, challenge yourself to control the way you respond to what's happening. That's where your power lies.

Your reaction to an event can hurt you more than the actual event.

—♡—♡—♡—♡—♡—♡—

The only thing you can control in this world is how you respond to what happens. You are in control of your inner space.

Letting go of disapproval of ourselves, is the key to unlocking the treasure of infinite love and peace present in our hearts.

We measure our self-worth against what society judges to be perfect. We judge ourselves as good or bad according to that, when in fact we are beyond labels.

When you look in the mirror, try
to look beyond the story you tell
yourself about yourself, and behold
a being whose purity is eternal.

"We cannot inspire others by trying to be perfect.
We can only inspire others by showing how
compassionately we embrace
our imperfections."
- Francois

Meditation is not about forcing the mind and emotions to stop...

Meditation is allowing the mind and emotions to express fully without identifying with them.

ALLOWING = LOVE

"Quiet the mind, and the soul will speak."- Ma Jaya Sati Bhagavati

When meditation is mastered, the mind is unwavering like the flame of a candle in a windless place." - Bhagavad Gita

When you own your breath, nobody can steal your peace.

"Suffering is due to our disconnection with the inner soul. Meditation is establishing that connection." - Amit Ray

"You have a treasure within you that is infinitely greater than anything the world can offer. Wisdom comes with the ability to be still. Just look and listen. No more is needed." - Eckhart Tolle

HOW TO MEDITATE

1 FIND A QUIET SPOT	**2 SIT COMFORTABLY**	**3 FOCUS ON YOUR BREATHING**
Pick any place and time where you won't be disturbed for a few minutes.	Sit cross-legged on the floor or on a chair if preferred.	Pay attention to the movement of your chest, mouth, and belly.
4 FEEL YOUR BREATH GOING IN AND OUT	**5 NOTICE THOUGHTS THAT ARISE**	**6 GENTLY RETURN YOUR BREATH**
Inhale Exhale	It's natural for the mind to be full of thoughts. Do not fight them. Instead, observe them.	Calmly let the thoughts pass and come back to the present by focusing on the breathing.
7 AIM FOR FIVE MINUTES	**8 PRACTICE EVERYDAY**	**9 MAKE PROGRESS PATIENTLY**
If that's too much, start with one minute. A timer prevents the need to check a clock or watch.	Concentrate on making this a habit	Sit patiently and observe your thoughts and relax in the present.

I LOVE MY BODY

Hey Girl, Please be kind to your body. It loves you more than anyone or anything in this world. It fixes every cut, every wound, every broken bone, and fights off so many illnesses, sometimes without you even knowing about it. Even when you punish it. It is still there for you, struggling to keep you alive, keep you healthy and breathing. Your body is an ocean full of love. So, please be kind to it. It's doing the very best it can.

—♡—♡—♡—♡—♡—♡—

You are not too fat or too skinny. You are not too old or too wrinkly. Your nose isn't too big and your boobs aren't too small. You are not ugly or stupid. This body of yours no matter what shape or size has carried you around your whole life. It's taken you to places, enabled you to explore the world. Picked you up when you've fallen down.

Hey Girl, make a promise to yourself to start appreciating what your body CAN do and stop focusing on what it can't. Promise me to stop judging every angle and every curve and every pound and every meal. If we make self-love or body acceptance conditional, the truth is we will never be happy with ourselves. The reality is that our bodies are constantly changing. If we base our self-worth on something as ever-changing as our bodies, we will forever be on the emotional roller coaster of body obsession and shame.

_ / _ / _

It's all about accepting yourself the way you are. My body is not yours to critique and discuss. My body is not yours for consumption. My body is my vessel. An archive of experiences. A weapon that has fought battles only I understand. A library of love, pain, struggle, victory, and mystery. You eyes cannot define all it has endured. Do not place value upon my body, place it upon my being. - Sophie Lewis

—♡—♡—♡—♡—♡—♡—

Dear Body

I'm sorry for the hurtful things I 've said,
you are always there protecting and nourishing me.
I'm sorry for all the times I judged you,
how I've always tried to change you or alter you
rather than understand and respect you.
I'm sorry for punishing you even though all you
wanted was to be fed and healthy.
Dear body, thank you for loving me even when
I didn't love you back.
I promise from today on, I will listen and act
with love, and nourish you because
I love you and respect you.
Dear body, thank you.

And I said to my

body, softly,

"I want to be your friend."

it took a long breath,

and replied,

"I have been waiting

my whole life

for this."

-Nayyirah Waheed

When you look in the mirror, do you accept
or reject yourself? If you reject yourself,
what are the thoughts that create the
feeling of being rejected? You have a choice not
to believe these thoughts.
Are these thoughts true? Who told you they were true?
Question the validity of why you should continue
believing these thoughts? Why keep suffering?

Ask yourself:
"Who would I be
without these
thoughts?"
- Byron Katie

THE TOXIC EFFECTS OF NEGATIVE SELF-TALK

As part of your self-love journey, pay attention to the stories you tell yourself. Learn to identify your thoughts: Is this thought true, or is it just a warped or a false story you are telling yourself? Thinking negative things about yourself may feel like astute observations, but your thoughts and feelings about yourself can definitely not be considered accurate information. Your thoughts can be skewed like everyone else's, subject to biases and the influence of your moods. Take a moment to check the validity of the story. Sometimes sharing a thought with another person can help you identify whether it's accurate. Whether you are checking in with yourself or someone else, start getting in the habit of challenging these inaccurate stories.

Many of us are terrified of being rejected because of experiences in our past. We navigate around rejection because the idea of opening that wound scares us. But fear of rejection can hold us back; it stops us from taking risks and being vulnerable, even when we might benefit from doing so. So try this. Think of asking someone for a favor that you are almost certain will result in a no. It could be something as small as requesting a free drink or a free ticket for a show. You will hear no, and you will be okay! Teaching yourself how to live with rejection is an crucial step in opening yourself up to new experiences with unpredictable outcomes.

You don't need to add more spiritual knowledge to be enlightened. Subtract all the good or bad opinions you have about yourself, and let the inner silence, the space of no judgement reveal who you truly are.

"You don't have to learn how to love yourself. You just have to remember there was nothing wrong. With you to begin with. You just have to come home."
- Nayyirah Waheed

HEALTH AFFIRMATIONS

- I am healthy and full of energy.
- I attract good and positive energy to
mind, body, and soul.
- The universe helps me achieve beautiful levels
of health and wellness.
- I enjoy existing in a natural state of well-being.
- I welcome positive and healthy energy
with open arms.
- Every day is an opportunity to enjoy new
levels of energy and well-being.
- I choose to let my natural, glorious, and
healthy energy shine.
- It comes naturally for me to feel
good and healthy.
- I am a magnet for healthy, uplifting, and
empowering energy.

I LIVE A LIFE OF PURPOSE

Strive for progress not perfection.

Hey Girl, Your life's purpose is to develop a sense of higher self. Trust yourself and others, and trust in the process of your life, so that you can feel safe enough to open up and share your inner beauty and wisdom with the world. The best day of your life is the one on which you decide your life is your own. No apologies or excuses. No one to lean on, rely on, or blame. The gift is yours.

It is an amazing journey—and, you alone are responsible for the quality of it. This is the day your life really begins. A meaningful life is not being rich, popular, highly educated, or perfect. It's about being real, humble, able to share ourselves and touch the lives of others.

Your life has purpose.
Your story is important.
Your dreams count.
Your voice matters.
You were born to make an impact.

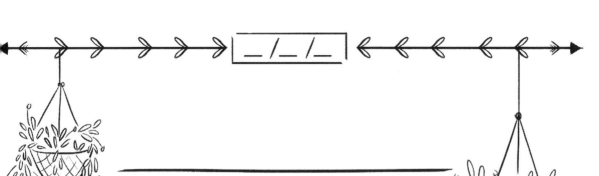

Positive Affirmations for Inner Peace

- I will stop worrying about everything.

- I will live a healthy lifestyle.

- I will stop dwelling on the past.

- I will forgive myself and others.

- I am becoming more at ease with myself.

- I will be more honest with myself.

- I will do what I love to do.

- I will take things on with a gentle approach.

- I will stop feeling the need to control everything.

- I will let life play out on its own.

I AM AUTHENTIC

"To be authentic, we must cultivate the courage to be imperfect — and vulnerable. We have to believe that we are fundamentally worthy of love and acceptance, just as we are. I've learned that there is no better way to invite more grace, gratitude and joy into our lives than by mindfully practicing authenticity."- Brené Brown

Hey Girl! Authenticity is when you say and do things you actually believe. It is to knowing who you are and being brave enough to accept it and live it. When you stop pretending to be anything other than who you truly are, and instead, put all of that energy into being yourself, your life will transform. You won't have to worry about
fitting in, because you will be focused on simply being YOU! When you stop pretending to be anyone else, you will become your truest self and who you were meant to be. Authenticity is a practice—a conscious choice of how we choose to live. It's about being honest with your choice, the choice to let our true self be seen.

Hey Girl! Try being authentic... be completely yourself so that everyone else feels safe to be themselves too. It takes courage to be yourself in a world where you are constantly told that who you are isn't enough. Authenticity is about presence, living in the moment with conviction and confidence and staying true to yourself. An authentic person puts the people around them at ease, like a comforting, old friend who welcomes us in and makes us feel at home.

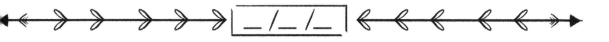

My Attributes
Let's be honest. We judge everybody we meet. We all do.
How about judging yourself for a change?

	Sometimes	Mostly	Always
Honest			
Generous			
Forgiving			
Happy			
Loyal			
Unique			
Humorous			
Intelligent			
Accomodating			
Talented			
Confident			
Humble			
Loving			
Tolerant			
Spontaneous			
Resilient			
Creative			
Fashionable			
Kind			
Self-loving			

There is nothing more rare, nor more beautiful, than a girl being unapologetically herself; comfortable in her perfect imperfection. To me, that is the true essence of beauty.

-Steve Maraboli

IMAGINE
That for once you
could reveal the
truth about how
you really feel.
What would we learn?

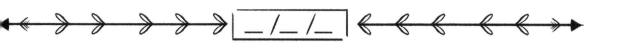

_ /_ /_

THINK OF A TIME WHEN YOU
LONGED TO EXPRESS SOMETHING
IN YOUR HEART BUT WERE AFRAID
TO. WHAT WAS IT?

_____

_____

_____

_____

_____

_____

_____

_____

_____

_____

_____

_____

_____

_____

_____

_____

DISCOVERING YOUR OWN IDENTITY

SURRENDER
Realize that life is only defined by the limits we place on ourselves. Go with the flow.

POTENTIAL
Realize our true potential and stop at nothing to follow our dreams.

LESSONS
Take what we have learned from the past, and use this to design our future.

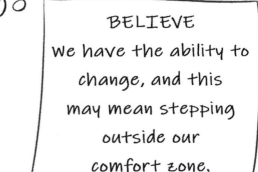

BELIEVE
We have the ability to change, and this may mean stepping outside our comfort zone.

LOOK INWARD
Look inside ourselves for the answers to all our questions.

REMEMBER
Our ability to be who we want to be is limitless.

CHANGE & GROW
Embrace it even if it's scary and uncertain. If we don't try, we won't know.

FUTURE
Create what we want by visualising it and then designing it the way we see it happening.

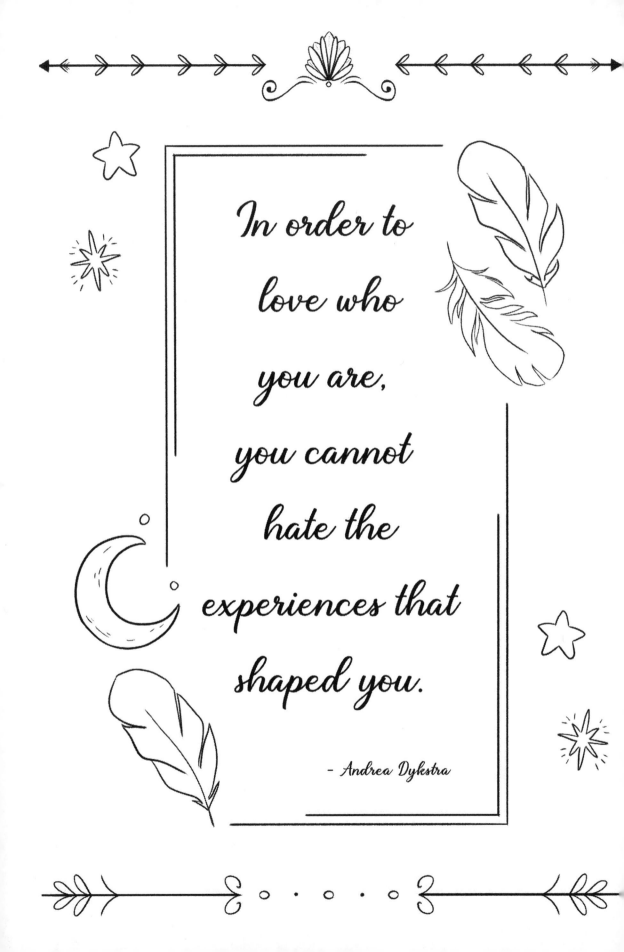

In order to
love who
you are,
you cannot
hate the
experiences that
shaped you.

- Andrea Dykstra

I RELEASE SHAME

Silencing Shame

Shame is learned. We are not born with shame. So when you think, "I am not good enough", ask yourself, where did I learn this from?

Hey Girl! When you are shamed as a child, that shame becomes internalized into a lack of self-worth. Unlike guilt, which is the feeling of doing something wrong; shame is the feeling of being something wrong. It is that voice that says "I am not good enough." You end up believing that you are flawed and unworthy of the connection you so desperately seek. This often causes an insatiable need for approval from others and a need to feel like you belong.

"When we experience shame, we feel disconnected and desperate for worthiness. Full of shame or the fear of shame, we are more likely to engage in self-destructive behaviors and to attack or shame others. In fact, shame is related to violence, aggression, depression, addiction, eating disorders, and bullying." -Bene Brown

Women who struggle with self-worth and insecurity often find them-selves in the chaser role. Bonding from a place of shame can make you physically and emotionally ill. For one thing, bonding with others over the parts of yourself that you feel ashamed of puts you in victim-mode. If you bond while in victim-mode, eventually, these relationships backfire leading to deeper feelings of self-hatred and even self-abuse. This dynamic can show up in a work situation, family relationship, friendship, or with a romantic partner.

The desire to feel special and have someone reassure us of our worth creates a pattern in which we chase others. This pattern may look like continually reaching out, smothering with attention, and engaging in ways to get noticed when the other person does not respond. Often, the chased pulls away, leaving us to feel even more rejected and insecure.

The shadows of shame can convince you that you need to pretend in order to receive validation from others. But any validation you end up receiving is bittersweet. Although it feels good, it doesn't feel real, because you haven't been your authentic self. Consider the ways in which the shadows of shame encourage you to be fake. What would it be like to take off the mask and let others see you as you are?

When you learn that the hot coal that someone throws at you does not have anything to do with you, it allows
you to choose whether or not to catch it, plant it, or drop it?

STEPS FOR RELEASING SHAME

- Identify the true source of shame.
- Open your heart: Shame thrives in darkness and secrecy.
- Redirect your thoughts to a more positive place.
- Acknowledge your higher self
- Learn mindfulness skills.
- Identify where in your body you feel the shame?
- Use affirmations to practice self-compassion.
- Know that releasing shame takes time.
- Self-compassion: Compassion is the direct inverse of shame.
- Go further with self-forgiveness.
- Own your story: In order to release your shame you have to be willing to take responsibility for yourself and your circumstances.

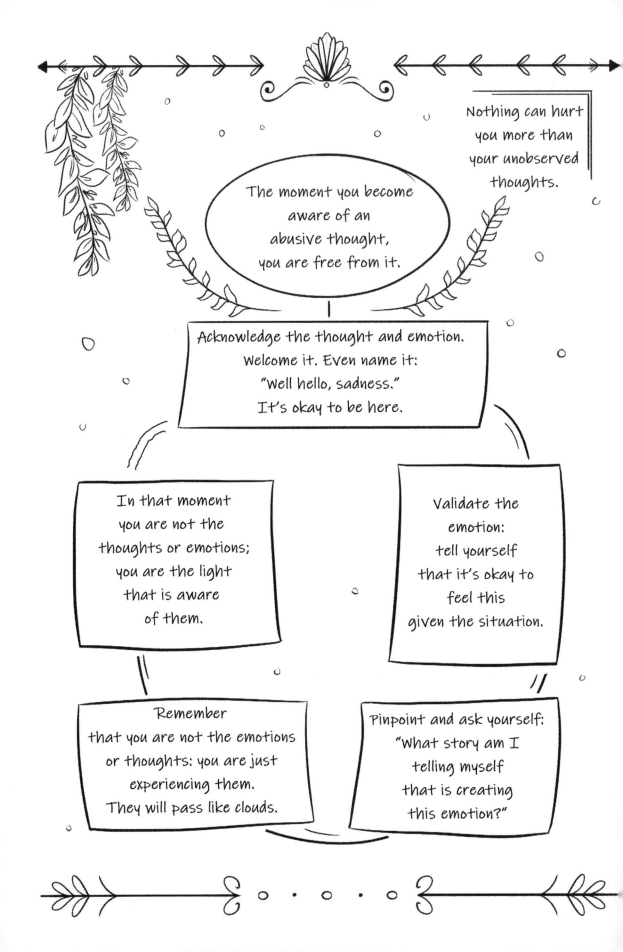

Nothing can hurt you more than your unobserved thoughts.

The moment you become aware of an abusive thought, you are free from it.

Acknowledge the thought and emotion. Welcome it. Even name it: "Well hello, sadness." It's okay to be here.

In that moment you are not the thoughts or emotions; you are the light that is aware of them.

Validate the emotion: tell yourself that it's okay to feel this given the situation.

Remember that you are not the emotions or thoughts: you are just experiencing them. They will pass like clouds.

Pinpoint and ask yourself: "What story am I telling myself that is creating this emotion?"

Talk about how you feel...
Even when it's tough to do.
Painful feelings often begin to dissolve
when you get them out of your system
and into the air.

—♥—♥—♥—♥—♥—♥—

We are all imperfectly perfect.
Our imperfections are what create
our uniqueness, and our uniqueness
is the best contribution
we can give to the planet.

Every morning, you have a new opportunity to become a happier version of yourself.

My future starts when
I wake up every morning.
Every day I find something
creative to do with my life.

– Miles Davis

I AM THE AUTHOR OF MY STORY

What if you had the power to write your own story? The story of how your life will be. Would you do it? Would you take charge of your story?

Hey Girl! You are the author of your own story. If you're stuck on the same page, remember at any moment you have the power to turn the page and start writing a new chapter. Your life is a book in progress, and you are the author. Get rid of the things that don't belong. Add more of the things that bring you happiness. Dream big and start writing your new adventure. Find the characters that are meant to help you on your journey. Embrace the middle chapters that are full of excitement and possibility. Write your own story because you are the only one who can. Write it with passion, with love! Try writing a good one.

No one else can tell your story, so tell it yourself.
No one else can write your story, so write it yourself.

Send love to all
who cross your path.

Every thought we think
is creating own future.
                    - Louise Hay

Tell the story of your family
Every family has a history.

Photo or sketch of your family

My family consists of:

_____

_____

_____

_____

_ / _ / _

My Family Story

_____
_____
_____
_____
_____
_____
_____
_____
_____
_____
_____
_____
_____
_____
_____
_____
_____
_____

Write your story!

_____

_____

_____

_____

_____

_____

_____

_____

_____

_____

_____

_____

_____

_____

_____

_____

_____

_____

_____

_____

_____

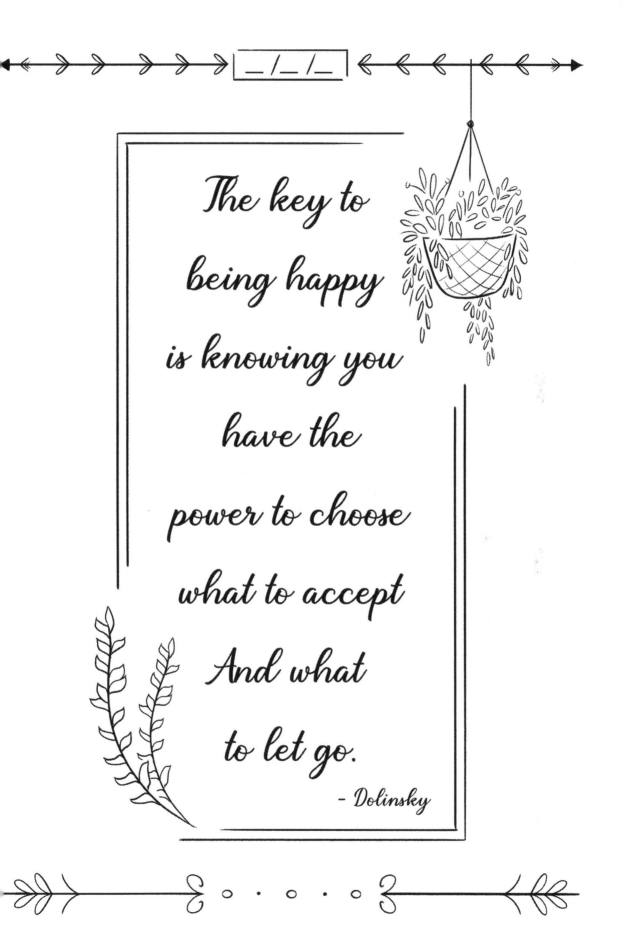

_ /_ /_

The key to
being happy
is knowing you
have the
power to choose
what to accept
And what
to let go.

— Dolinsky

I AM CONFIDENT

I am confident because I can accept who I am,
what I've done, and love myself for who I've become.

—♡—♡—♡—♡—♡—♡—

Hey Girl! The only one who gets to decide your worth is you.
It doesn't come from the things you own or number of friends
you have. It doesn't come from what someone else says you
are worth. It's called self-worth for a reason—it comes from you.

Your confidence comes from being youself and being proud of who
you are. It comes from being someone that you can count on and
someone you love. The outside things will change with time, but
that won't change who you are deep inside—beautiful, limitless,
wonderful, creative, strong, capable—and that is where
your worth comes from.

TWO TYPES OF CONFIDENCE

My self value
comes from
the world.

My self value
comes from
within.

Confidence is not
"They will like me."

Confidence is
"I'll be fine if they don't."

Be the flawed, quirky, unique, beautiful & magical person that you are!

I CHOOSE MY THOUGHTS

I have the power to control my thoughts.
I am in charge of how I feel.
My thoughts shape my vision.
I see what I choose to see.

Hey Girl! Your happiness depends on the quality of your thoughts. Choose your thoughts wisely, for they are the energy that shapes your life. Just imagine your mind is like a garden and your thoughts are the seeds. You get to choose which seeds you plant in it. You can choose to plant love, hope, and abundance, or you can plant the seeds of anxiety, fear, and jealousy. We become what we give our time and attention to. When you fill your mind with thoughts of kindness, love, faith, hope, and joy, your reality will become all of those things. You will start to see love, hope, and kindness in the world. You will begin to feel positive as you go about your day. You will notice more of the little joys of life. You've tried listening to your fears and doubts, and they have never brought you happiness. It's time to start choosing love. It's time to start believing in yourself. Learn how to choose your thoughts the way you choose your clothes each day.

Your mind is a very powerful thing.
When you choose to fill it with positive thoughts,
your life will start to change.

_ /_ /_

"We are what our
thoughts have made us;
so take care about
what you think.
Words are secondary.
Thoughts live;
they travel far."

- Swami Vivekananda

You are not your thoughts unless you actually choose them.
No need to dwell on them, act on them, fight with them,
or try to avoid them. Take notice and let them go.

Instead of: Try:
I'm a mess.   I am human.
I'm a failure.   I'm learning.
Why is this happening?   What is it teaching me?

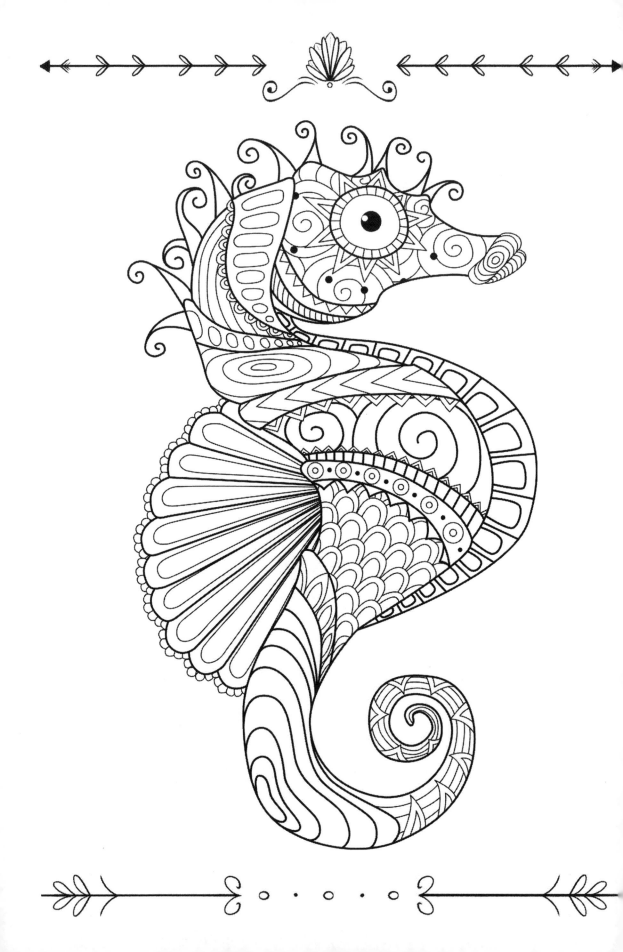

Happiness
is the new rich.
Inner peace is
the new success.
Health is the
new wealth.
Kindness is
the new cool.

MY FEELINGS

Color the feelings on this page according to the chart.

COLOR	I FEEL THIS WAY...
green	Often
blue	Sometimes
yellow	Never/Hardly Ever

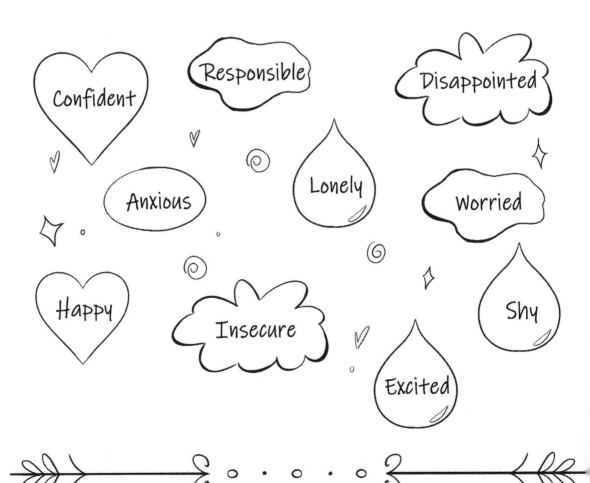

Give yourself
permission
to have fun!

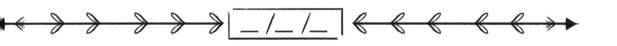

I CELEBRATE LIFE

I bring joy to this world!

Everyday of your life is a special occasion.
Cherish every moment!

—♡—♡—♡—♡—♡—♡—

Hey Girl! You are meant to fill life with all the wonderful things that fill your heart with joy. You are meant to live in a way that lights your soul from the inside out. Celebrate your big and little wins. Grow every day! Nourish yourself! Compliment others whenever you can. Make art.

Life is meant to be lived. Take a deep breath of fresh air. Go for a walk under the open blue sky. Explore the wild—hug trees, watch animals, enjoy the sunrise. Enjoy the small things life has to offer. Learn to appreciate quiet moments. Celebrate your health, your strength, your smile, your life.

If you fuel your journey on the opinions of others, you are going to run out of gas.

- Steve Maraboli

I AM STRONG. I DREAM BIG. I DO MY BEST!

Magic happens when you do not give up, even though you want to. The universe often falls in love with a stubborn heart. -J.M.Storm

Fear is nothing more than an obstacle that stands in the way of progress.

Hey Girl, Please remember, nothing is permanent. You're not trapped. You have choices. Think of new ideas, make new plans, learn something new, imagine new thoughts, take new actions, meet new people, form new habits. All that matters is that you decide today and never look back. Fear is nothing more than an obstacle that stands in the way of progress. In overcoming our fears, we can move forward, become stronger, and develop wisdom within ourselves.

Hey Girl! You got this! Success is not built on success. It's built on failure. It's built on frustration. It's built on not giving up. Try your best with no expectation and then let the universe take care of it.

Let's keep trying!. Keep believing!
Never give up. Your day will come.

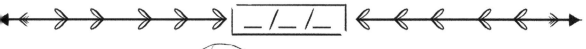

Feel the fear,
process it,
and do what you
need to achieve
what you've set out
for yourself.

- Lewis Howes

Say this:
I am a winner.
I am capable of everything I set my mind to.
I take every setback and use it to my advantage.

I am confident in who I am.
I am confident in what I have to offer the world.
I am confident in my abilities and purpose.

I am not held back by fear,
doubt, or disappointment.

I am ready to
contribute something beautiful
and meaningful to this world.

_ _ / _ _ / _ _

Seek that which makes your mind sing, Your body sing, Your heart sing, Your spirit sing!

-Tabaash

CREATE YOUR DREAM LIFE

If you could have any job in the world, what would it be and why?

What does happiness mean to you?

If you could travel anywhere in the world where would it be and why?

_ /_ /_

If you had three wishes, what would you wish for?

What do you feel most passionate about and why?

Name five things you do well.

What do you need more of in your life?

Self-Care Ideas

Spiritual Self-Care

- Spend time in nature
- Meditate
- Pray
- Recognize the things that give meaning to your life
- Act in accordance with your morals and values
- Set aside time for thought and reflection
- Participate in a cause that is important to you
- Appreciate art that is inspiring to you
  (e.g. music, film, literature)

Hey Girl! You are incredible. You make this world a little bit more wonderful. You have so much potential and so many things left to do. It is time to give that lovely soul of yours the words she's been longing to hold onto. Trust the process, and cherish whatever comes, because your hands and your heart will not lie to you; you'll know just what to say.

Write a love letter to yourself

_____

_____

_____

_____

_____

_____

_____

_____

_____

_____

_____

_____

_____

_____

_____

Remember this ...

Be inspired by the success of others.

It's okay to ask for help.

You are what you choose to be.

Your boundaries are important and worth respect.

You are important and you matter.

Connect with the universe.

Believe in yourself.

_ / _ / _

Your mistakes don't define you.

You are worthy of great things.

You are enough.

You are allowed to say no.

You can overcome challenges.

Productivity doesn't define your worth.

Your wants and needs are valid.

I FORGIVE. FORGIVENESS IS AN ACT OF SELF-LOVE

Forgive others not because they deserve
forgiveness but because you deserve peace. -JLH

Hey Girl! It took me a great deal of time to realize what it meant to forgive someone. I always contemplated how could I forgive someone who hurt me. But after a lot of soul-searching, I realized that forgiveness is not about accepting or excusing someone's behavior. It's about letting it go and preventing it from disrupting your inner peace. Sometimes people hurt each other. It happens to all of us. Purposely or accidentally, regretfully or not. It's a part of what we are as people. The beauty is that we have the ability to let go, heal, and forgive. Forgiveness is a catalyst creating the atmosphere necessary for a fresh start and a new beginning.

All of us have wounds: wounds of rejection, loss, neglect, abandonment, betrayal, or abuse. Show yourself love by focusing on healing your wounds. The first step is becoming aware of them. The next step is to reach out and ask for help. A trusted friend, a family member, or even a stranger who's a wise and compassionate listener can be the remedy you need to help you heal.

Holding a grudge doesn't make you strong;
it makes you bitter.
Forgiving doesn't make you weak;
it sets you free.

Be like a tree
and let the
dead leaves drop.
- Rumi

Every experience
is an opportunity
to awaken.

"If you do not forgive yourself, the shame you carry
will compel you to continue to act in harmful ways
toward others and yourself." - Beverly Engel

IMAGINE
That you could forgive
someone who hurt you.

How would your life change?

_____

_____

_____

_____

_____

_____

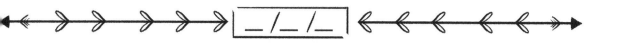

_ _ / _ _ / _ _

My Letter of Apology

Dear _____

I would like to apologize for _____

_____

This was wrong because _____

_____

I am sure it made you feel _____

Next time, I will make the better choice to _____

_____

I promise that from now on, I'll be kind and respectful at all times. I am sorry for my actions, and I am glad you are my friend!

Sincerely,

_____

All your life, everything that ever happened — even the hard stuff — made you into the incredible person you are.

I EMBRACE MY IMPERFECT LIFE

Hey Girl! People change, so you can learn to let go. Things go wrong, so you can appreciate them when they're right. If you believe lies, you eventually learn to trust no one but yourself. And sometimes good things fall apart, so better things can come together.

Someone once told me to always live for the little things in life. Live for sunrises and sunsets, when you see colors in the sky that don't usually belong. Live for road trips and bike rides with music in your ears and wind in your hair. Live for the days when you are surrounded by your favorite people who make you realize the world is not a cold harsh place. Live for the little things, because they will make you realize that this is what life is about. This is what it means to be alive.

—♥—♥—♥—♥—♥—♥—

Hey Girl! I wish for you an imperfect life and all the wonder it can bring... the wealth that comes from knowing loss, the tears that find their way to laughter, the joy that grows after the rain, and the love, felt deepest, by those who have been carved by pain. I hope that you can value this imperfection, hold on to it, so it gives you such comfort that you will embrace the beauty of all imperfect lives that surround you. Then you will be free to step out of your own imperfect heart, you will have truly lived. - Jodi Hills

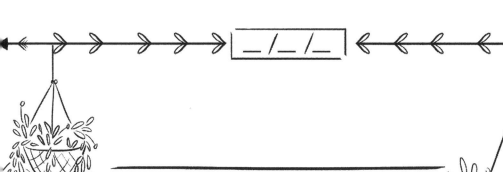

12 things to always remember:

1. The past can't be changed.

2. Opinions don't define your reality.

3. Everyone's journey is different.

4. Judgments are not about you.

5. Overthinking will lead to sadness.

6. Happiness is found within.

7. Your thoughts affect your mood.

8. Smiles are contagious.

9. Kindness is free.

10. It's okay to let go and move on.

11. What goes around, comes around.

12. Things always get better with time.

Breath by breath,

let go of the expectation,

fear, regret, and frustration.

Let go of the need for

constant approval.

You don't need

any of it.

I RELEASE SELF-DOUBT

Hey Girl, Learning to trust myself helps build my confidence and resilience. It helps me feel comfortable in my own skin. Trusting myself requires me to learn how to become quiet so I can hear that small voice inside that's there to guide me towards my soul's purpose. Self-belief can also mean self-reliance. When I follow through with commitments I've made to myself, it builds trust and releases self-doubt because I know I can count on myself to follow through. Through small steps like these I can strengthen the trust I have in myself in a long-lasting and powerful way.

When I trust myself, I feel comfortable speaking up and feel safe exploring new ideas. Trusting myself also means being honest and authentic and taking full responsibility for my life. When I trust myself, I feel whole and aligned.

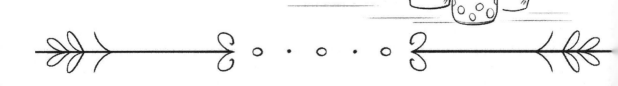

Sometimes it is not the lack of ability but the lack of confidence that prevents us from achieving what we really want. Sometimes it's doable, but self-doubt makes it impossible.

—♡—♡—♡—♡—♡—♡—

Whenever you find yourself doubting how far you can go, just remember how far you have come. Remember everything you have faced, all the battles you have won, and all the fears you have overcome.

SELF-DOUBT ASSESSMENT

True or False

I often think negative, catastrophic thoughts that start with "what if..."

_____

_____

_____

I believe I have failed many times.

_____

_____

_____

I worry about what others will think of me.

_____

_____

_____

I am hesitant to try new things due to fear of failure.

_____

_____

_____

I do not like to try new things.

_____

_____

_____

I replay conversations and think of things I could have said better.

_____

I believe that others will not like me.

_____

_____

I am afraid to go outside my comfort zone.

_____

_____

I start thinking negatively even before trying something new.

_____

_____

I often believe that I am not good enough.

_____

_____

I am often afraid of making mistakes.

_____

_____

I do not like to try something new unless I am good at it.

_____

_____

GRASS IS GREENER ON MY SIDE TOO!

I am inspired by the success of others.

—♡—♡—♡—♡—♡—♡—

"When you are content to be simply yourself and don't compare or compete, you will find respect." - Lao Tzu

Hey Girl! Every minute you spend wishing you had someone else's life is a minute spent wasting yours. There will always be someone who has a little more than you, and there will always be someone who has less. Stop comparing. Start accepting where you are right now. Because you won't ever be happy if you don't learn to love your imperfect, everyday life. The only person you should try to beat is the person you were yesterday.

Hey Girl! Don't compare your journey with others. We are all walking our own unique path. Comparison kills creativity. There is room for you. Nobody has your voice, your experience, or your mind. Happiness is found when you stop comparing yourself to others.

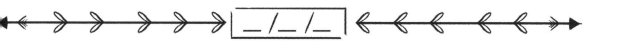

THE GAME OF COMPARISON

I am left feeling empty and incomplete.

Enough is never enough. Satisfaction is fleeting.

Everyone is a competitor, and I'm either winning or losing.

I've become blind to the gifts I already have.

—♡—♡—♡—♡—♡—♡—

Comparsion should be when I see the gap between who I am now and who I want to become in the future.

SELF-IMPROVEMENT

WHAT DO I WANT TO LEARN OVER THE NEXT SIX MONTHS?

HOW DO I WANT TO IMPROVE?

- An understanding of who I am and how I work
- An understanding of others
- An increase in my self-love and self-worth
- Better communication
- How to have better relationships with the people in my life
- Better self-control and how to manage:
  - My behaviors
  - My emotions
  - My thoughts
- How to reframe:
  - My thoughts (i.e. negative to positive)
  - My perceptions (my interpretation of situations)

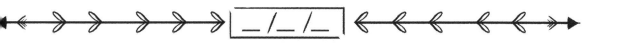

- How to improve my beliefs and mindset:
    - Remove limiting beliefs
    - Adopt a growth mindset
- How to grow my self-confidence:
    - Increase my self-esteem
    - Be more courageous
- How to accept reality, circumstances, and other people
- How to respect the boundaries of others
- How to heal from past wounds
- How to set boundaries
- How to let go
- Other (please specify)

_____
_____
_____
_____
_____
_____
_____
_____
_____

When stressed out or in doubt
look within.

INTUITION
is the ability to hear my own inner voice

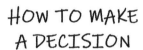

HOW TO MAKE A DECISION

1. Slow down, breathe.

2. Check in with your whole body. What is your gut feeling? Is your jaw tight?

3. What would your truest self do?

4. Know that we can learn from all decisions even the stupid ones.

I FOLLOW MY INTUITION

I trust the voice in my heart.

Listen to your own voice, your own soul.
Too many people listen to the noise of
the world, instead of themselves.
Deep inside, you know what you want.
Let no one decide that for you. - Leon Brown

Hey Girl! If something excites you and scares you at the same time, it perhaps means you should do it. Have the courage to follow your heart and your instinct. Let your heart guide you when you're lost. Follow it wherever it may lead.

Listen to advice, but follow your heart and your dreams. Let no one tell you that they're silly or foolish. If something is important to you, pursue it. You deserve to be happy.

Try following your heart instead of your doubts and fears, and you will find the people and places that are truly meant for you.

If you obsess over whether you are making the right decision, you are basically assuming that the universe will reward you for one thing and punish you for another.

The universe has no fixed agenda, it works around that decision. There is no right or wrong, only a series of possibilities that shift with each thought, feeling, and action you experience.

Look closely at the
present you are
constructing. It should
look like the future
you are dreaming.
Start telling the universe
what you want instead
of what you don't want.
If you can dream it,
you can do it.
Open your wings
and fly!

POWERFUL MORNING
affirmations

1   I have everything I need to face every
    challenge that comes.

2   I let go of negative, limiting beliefs that
    have held me back.

3   I trust my intuition to help me make wise
    decisions and take decisive action.

4   I have the power to create all the success
    and abundance I desire.

5   I feel calm, confident, and powerful as I
    face new challenges.

6   I celebrate every win with gratitude and
    joy.

7   I learn from every mistake and failure,
    so I can do better as I move forward.

8   My actions are intentional, and they lead
    me closer to my goals.

9   Confidence is second nature to me. I know
    I have what it takes to succeed.

10 Today, I abandon my old habits and adopt
    new, more empowering ones.

Let's talk about 11 habits of successful girls!

1. They live in a state of gratitude.

2. They have the power to control their mind and thoughts.

3. They educate themselves.

4. They make mistakes, learn from them, and move on.

5. They know the importance of self-care and health.

6. They know the importance of being independent.

7. They smile and laugh a lot.

8. They make goals and stick to them with hard work and perseverance.

9. They support their friends and enjoy their success.

10. They treat others with kindness.

11. They are authentic.

Hey Girl I hope you enjoyed going through this journal and found some value in my suggestions.

If you would like to get in touch with me, please email me PenMagicBooks@gmail.com

With love and appreciation,
Pragya Tomar

Made in the USA
Las Vegas, NV
17 October 2022

57455697R00090